About Educational Kinesiology (Edu-K)

This book has been published under the auspices of Brain Gym® International in Ventura, California, a nonprofit school that offers courses for teachers of Brain Gym®, Vision Gym®, and other Edu-K processes. Edu-K stands for education (the process of drawing out learning) and kinesiology (the study of movement). For Edu-K teachers, movement is the door to learning! Edu-K is based on the research and professional experience of Paul E. Dennison, Ph.D., an educator who has over the past thirty years introduced an entirely new method of teaching: one that uses simple body movements to activate whole-brain potential.

The Edu-K processes, used in homes, schools, and businesses worldwide, were introduced in German-speaking countries by the Institute for Applied Kinesiology in Freiburg, Germany, in 1983. *The Learning Gym*, originally written in German, was first published in Austria in 1992, under the title *Lerngymnastik*. All of the Brain Gym activities included are from the book *Brain Gym*, which has been translated into more than forty languages. The alternative to the Positive Points movement, shown on page 17, was adapted from a process taught in the course Edu-K in Depth: Seven Dimensions of Intelligence.

For more information, or for a comprehensive description of courses, contact:

Brain Gym® International
1575 Spinnaker Drive, Suite 204B
Ventura, CA 93001
Telephone: (805) 658-7942 • Fax: (805) 650-0524
edukfd@earthlink.net • www.braingym.org

German version copyright 1992
by hpt-Verlagsgesellschaft m.b.H. & Co. KG, Vienna: ISBN 3-7004-0231-7
English translation copyright 1996 and 2004
by Gail E. Dennison and Paul E. Dennison, Ph.D.
Original art by Erich Ballinger
All Brain Gym® movements are from the book *Brain Gym®*
by Dennison and Dennison, and are used by permission of the authors.

ISBN 0-942143-09-4

Erich Ballinger

The Learning Gym

**Fun-to-Do Activities
for Success at School**

Brain Gym®

Brings it together ©

Edu-Kinesthetics, Inc.

What? You too . . .

. . . find reading and learning a struggle, and you're having a hard time at school? It may not be much comfort to you, but there are many other kids facing the same challenges. Anyway, you probably don't need comforting as much as you need some practical help.

And here's the help you need: the Learning Gym! You might ask, "What can I possibly do to get more ready to learn than I already am?" Well, your brain (where you do your learning) is divided into two hemispheres or sides, and each side helps you in different ways. Reading and learning happen easily only when both sides of the brain work together. And that cooperation between your two brain hemispheres is exactly what you can achieve at the Learning Gym. You might not

become a star pupil overnight . . . yet if you're patient and do the movements every day, you'll soon find that school isn't hard for you any more. And if you keep on practicing regularly, you'll find that the success you've been looking for comes to you easily.

The activities in this book can calm you (help you to concentrate and to get over

any nervousness or fear of not doing well) at the same time that they energize you (wake you up

and help you with reading and learning). Thinking and remembering is easier when your body has all the water it needs, so keep some cool, fresh water always close by, and take little sips of it just as often as you want.

The Learning Gym makes learning fun. In fact, the more you enjoy these movements, the more you will learn. And the exercises are easy, too. Did you ever hear yourself say, "I can't do it!"? Before long, you're going to be saying, "Of course I can learn to do that. I'll just do my Learning Gym exercises, and then give it a whirl!"

The next page is for parents and teachers. That is to say, it's . . .

For Those Who Want to Know More

With the Brain Gym movements (the basis for this Learning Gym book), Dr. Dennison has created an easy-to-use method to help children learn to their full potential. And, through the Educational Kinesiology Foundation in California, instructors around the world are certified to teach the complete Brain Gym program. A few of the key Brain Gym activities are included in this book, to get children started on their own.

The Brain Gym method is based in part on scientific findings about the nature of the human brain, a complex organ made up of the cerebral cortex and separate structures beneath it. For purposes of simplicity, we will refer here only to the left and right hemispheres of the cortex. One hemisphere of the brain (in most people, the left half) controls the functions of analyzing and organizing, and is chiefly responsible for our short-term or working memory. The other hemisphere functions integrally, pictorially, and emotionally, and is chiefly responsible for our access to long-term memory. The left side of the brain controls the muscles of the right side of the body, while it's the right side of the brain that's active when the left side of the body is moved. Brain Gym integrates the two sides of the brain for whole-brain learning. This integration is necessary because–at any age–stress, fear of failure, and a lack of self-confidence may cause one half of the brain to overwork and the other half to "switch itself off." We are then working to only half of our potential, and for a child this can lead to failure at school.

If a child with whom you're working finds the Cross Crawl (page 10) too difficult, we recommend Dennison Laterality Repatterning–a procedure that facilitates more automatic neurological integration. A simple guide to this process can be found in the book *Edu-K for Kids* by Dennison and Dennison.

Do you enjoy reading, writing, looking, or listening as much as you used to, or as much as you would like to? If not, you can do something about it–now! If you lightheartedly do the Brain Gym activities along with your child, this will make it even more fun, and you will have the added benefit of improving your own physical and mental abilities.

Brain Buttons

Are you tired? Worn out? Don't feel like getting started? Do this:

● Rub your Brain Buttons with the thumb and first finger of one hand. You'll find these "buttons" at the soft spots under your collarbone. As you rub them, move your eyes slowly back and forth, left to right and right to left.

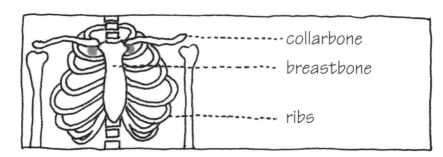

collarbone

breastbone

ribs

● While you rub your Brain Buttons, place the first finger and middle finger of your other hand over your belly button.

For Those Who Want to Know More:

By rubbing the Brain Buttons, we "wake up" neurological pathways related to eye-teaming, and activate the two sides of the brain to work together. This exercise can help children to:
• blend letter sounds
• avoid the reversing or transposing of letters
• read without losing their place or skipping words
• develop the healthy use of both eyes while reading

- While holding your Brain Buttons and belly button, rest your tongue against the roof of your mouth and think of something nice.

- After a minute, you'll feel refreshed and ready to go

Ahh! What a refreshing waker-upper!

Crossover Dancing

Would you like to dance? Let's put on some cheerful music and here we go!

● With your right hand, touch the opposite knee, as shown in the picture. Then you change sides, crossing your left hand over to your right knee, then your right hand back over to your left knee, and so on, back and forth. Loosen up, swing your arms, and stay in time with the music First your left . . . then right . . . left . . . right . . . that's it!

● As you do this dance, look all around you to relax and energize your eyes.

For Those Who Want to Know More:

Crossover Dancing is a Cross Crawl movement that stimulates both sides of the brain at once, increasing learning capability. In addition, this activity promotes:

- spatial awareness
- the ability to distinguish between left and right
- awareness of personal space and boundaries
- whole-body coordination
- binocular vision (flexible vision, using the two eyes as a team)

The music you choose can have a faster tempo for older or more experienced Crossover dancers.

After dancing, sit down in a comfortable position, clasp your hands together, and imagine how well both sides of your brain are now cooperating!

You'll find more Crossover dances on pages 28 and 29.

Earth Buttons and Space Buttons

When the inside of your head is like a thunderstorm—when you're restless or too excited—you can calm yourself down by doing these "lightning conductor" activities

● For the Earth Buttons part of this, touch the places above and below your lips with the first and

middle fingers of one hand. At the same time, place the first and middle fingers of your other hand over your belly button. Look up, then down, taking three deep breaths as you lightly rub the points near your lips.

Then reverse your hand positions. Look up and then down again, for three more deep breaths.

For Those Who Want To Know More:

The Earth Buttons and Space Buttons are important acupressure points. Activating these points helps bring about:

- focus and concentration
- a sense of grounding and gravity
- coordination of vision with equilibrium
- relaxation of the central nervous system
- decreased hyperactivity and distractibility

● These exercises are even more fun if you hum while you're doing them.

● Now for the Space Buttons! Cover your belly button with one hand again, and with the other hand gently rub where your tailbone starts (if you're not sure where your tailbone is, this picture will help you find it).

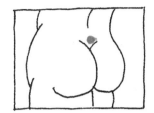

Take three deep breaths while doing this, and then reverse your hand positions for three more deep breaths. Now the weather inside your head should be fine again!

One more thing: Do the Brain Buttons before and after these other Buttons, to help you feel refreshed and relaxed at the same time.

mmm...!

This exercise looks a bit different when we elephants do it!

13

The Thinking Cap

Do you ever have trouble "getting" something you're listening to at school? Here's an ear-opening activity that can help.

Elephants are good listeners and have great memories. You can listen better and remember, too. Just unroll your ears—very gently, of course—any time you need to listen well.

- Using your thumbs and first fingers, slowly pull the edges of your ears out and backward, as if you wanted to open them.

For Those Who Want To Know More:

The Thinking Cap stimulates reflex points that enhance hearing and understanding. In this way:

- attentiveness is increased
- listening and speaking abilities are improved
- the memory is activated
- both the sounds and the meaning of speech are perceived

- Start at the tops of the ears and work down to your earlobes, unrolling them three or more times.

- After you've "opened" your ears, you'll be able to listen better and remember more of what you hear. After all, you don't want anyone telling you, "Wash out those ears!"

The Positive Points

● We're all sometimes afraid of certain things, like taking tests or making mistakes, yet fear makes it hard for us to think. It turns off the light in our heads, shorts out our circuits, cuts down our power. In a situation like this, all you have to do is reach for your "light switches"—your Positive Points—and the light in your mind will come on again!

● You'll find your Positive Points on your forehead, between your eyebrows and your hairline. They may feel like two low mounds or bumps.

● Hold your Positive Points when something is worrying you. It's a good thing to do just before you take a test.

● Touch these points gently with your fingertips, close your eyes, breathe deeply, and relax. Think of your fear, or remember something that happened to you that was hard. You'll find that troubles don't bother you so much any more.

For Those Who Want to Know More:
Touching the Positive Points brings circulation to the front of the brain, helping to balance emotional stress with a rational attitude, and thus making it more likely that a solution will be recognized. This activity:
- reduces stress and tension
- releases memory blocks ("It's on the tip of my tongue!")
- relaxes the eyes and increases eye-teaming skills
- helps one make objective decisions

(Note: The finger position on page 17 relaxes muscles that may contract involuntarily when a pen or pencil is held.)

- Do Positive Points for one minute, or until "the light comes on."
- You can also ask someone else to hold your Positive Points for you. That way, it's easier for you to relax.
- Touch the nail of your ring finger with your thumb tip, as in this little picture, to get a similar relaxing effect (great when taking tests!).

Now my light is on!

17

Cook's Hook-ups

When you're tired or nervous, or you just can't concentrate, enjoy a Hook-up!

● Sit down as the boy in Picture 1 is doing. It's up to you whether you cross your left leg over your right or the other way around—just sit in the way that's more comfortable for you.

With your eyes open or closed, breathe in through your nose and touch your tongue to the roof of your mouth.

Now relax your tongue as you breathe out through your mouth.

For Those Who Want to Know More:

Cook's Hook-ups was developed by Wayne Cook, a specialist in the physics of electromagnetic force fields. Hook-ups is both a relaxing and an energizing activity. It especially promotes:

- emotional calm and self-esteem
- attentiveness
- deeper, more beneficial breathing
- quicker recovery from excessive exposure to TV, computer, or other overstimulation of the nervous system

● After about a minute, sit as the girl in Picture 2 is sitting. Let your fingertips touch as if you were holding a ball, and breathe deeply for one more minute.

● Well, how do you feel? Strong enough to uproot trees? That's great—but please leave the trees alone!

I feel as strong as a whole herd of elephants!

Picture 1   Picture 2

The Elephant

Imagine that you're an elephant, with big ears, a long trunk, and strong legs planted firmly on the ground. You're looking far into the distance, above the trees, for some of your elephant friends.

● Elephants often sway slowly from side to side. Copy them! Lay your ear against your shoulder and reach out your arm. Pretend that your arm is your trunk, attached firmly to your head.

● Swing your arm, your head, and the top half of your body slowly and loosely through the air, as if you're drawing a big figure 8 lying on its side. Do this three or more times.

For Those Who Want to Know More!

It's a proven fact that a connection exists between the muscles in the neck and the perception and differentiation of sounds. The effects of the Elephant exercise are that:

- the neck muscles are relaxed
- listening comprehension is enhanced
- auditory memory is sharpened
- speaking ability is improved
- the sense of balance is stimulated

- Start your figure 8 at the middle of the 8, then move upward to the left or the right. When you feel steady, let your eyes follow your fingers, looking beyond them into the distance. You may see a double image. That's O.K.!

- Do the Elephant three or more times with the other arm, too.

- Elephants get very thirsty. Sip some water after you swing and sway.

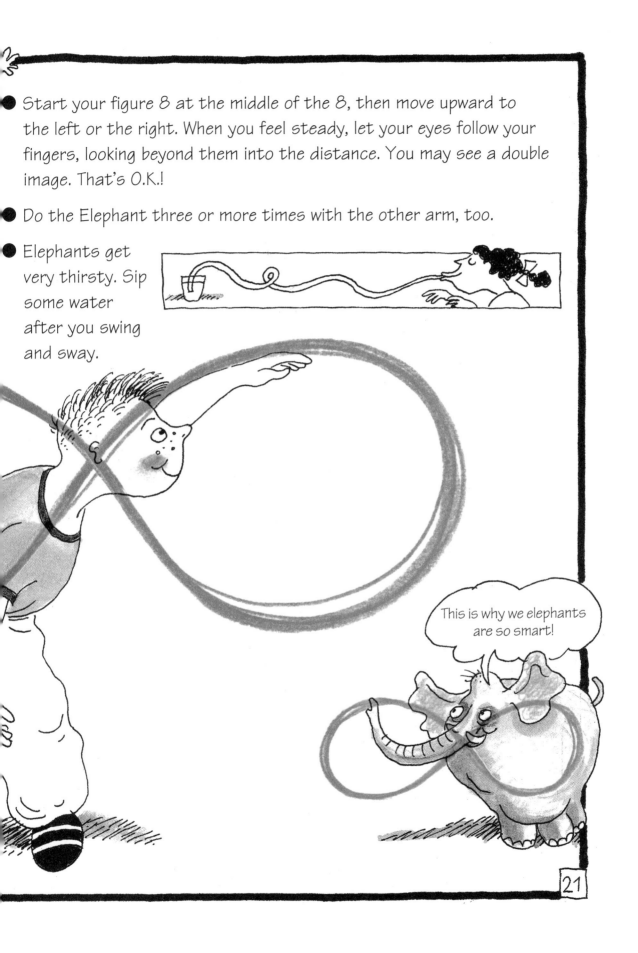

This is why we elephants are so smart!

Lazy 8s

If you get your b's and d's mixed up when you're reading and writing, here's a way to unmix them.

● Reach out with your writing hand and draw a big figure 8 lying on its 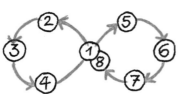 side in the air. Starting at the center, follow the upward movement of your hand with your eyes as you draw three or more 8s.

● Now draw the same kind of Lazy 8 with the other hand, three or more times, and then draw three or more Lazy 8s using both hands together.

● Draw your napping 8s slowly and loosely; they like to be nice and big.

● Begin the middle of each 8 right in front of your nose.

For Those Who Want to Know More:
The Lazy 8 is an easy and natural way to smoothly cross the visual midline that connects the left and right visual fields. This activity:

- facilitates eye-teaming skills
- eliminates the confusion of letters
- encourages the ability to recognize and distinguish symbols
- promotes the ability to write without stress
- improves the sense of balance and coordination

● Reach with your eyes and nose wherever your fingertips go.

● Do this exercise with music. You can even sing your Lazy 8 a lullaby, so that it can nap better:

Three, four, five . . . six, seven, eight—
my eight is not yet quite awake.
My eight still needs to finish his nap.
That's why he's wearing his little
night cap!

Three, four, five, six, seven, eight, my eight is not yet quite awake . . .

● Draw your napping 8 on a blackboard or on a big sheet of paper. How big can you make the 8? How little?

I like drawing the lying-down 8 while I'm lying down!

The Gravity Glider

Gravity naturally pulls us toward the earth, and in this movement, we let it! You can do the Gravity Glider while standing, like the children shown here, or sitting (the regular way, which is easier—and especially good if you've been sitting too long!).

- While sitting forward on your chair, cross your ankles and relax your knees. Raise your arms over your head, next to your ears, then let your head and arms hang forward.

- Let your arms and the top half of your body hang down loosely, keeping your neck relaxed and gliding your arms out in front of you.

- Come up again, head last, and gracefully raise your arms overhead.

- Do two more reaches, to the right and to the left, then cross your legs the other way and reach three times again.

- To do the standing variation, just cross your ankles and reach up and then forward, keeping your head down and your neck relaxed. Repeat to one side, then the other, as you did while sitting.

The only thing I like more is flying!

● Go ahead–give it your best! When you sit down again afterward, you'll feel as perky as the bird in the cuckoo clock!

Cuckoo!

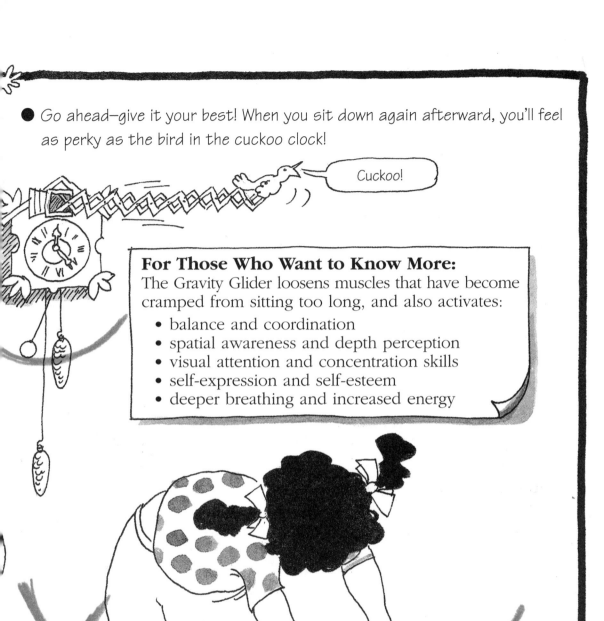

For Those Who Want to Know More:
The Gravity Glider loosens muscles that have become cramped from sitting too long, and also activates:
- balance and coordination
- spatial awareness and depth perception
- visual attention and concentration skills
- self-expression and self-esteem
- deeper breathing and increased energy

The Double Doodle

Drawing with both hands isn't hard at all!

● Do your first Double Doodle with empty hands–drawing in the air, like an orchestra conductor who's not using a baton. Listen to a piece of music and "conduct it," letting your hand movements mirror each other. Then do some more Double Doodles without music, starting out slowly, then going faster and faster.

● Now fasten a big piece of wrapping paper to the wall. Take two different-colored crayons, markers, colored pencils, or pieces of chalk, and hold one in each hand. Start with both colors in the middle of the paper, and draw two mirror-image designs, using both hands at the same time.

No need to be shy about it–off you go!

For Those Who Want to Know More:
It's not the final drawing that matters in this exercise; it's the action itself that's important. Drawing with both hands at once:
- activates hand-eye coordination and assists eye-teaming across the visual midline
- helps establish handedness–the consistent use of one hand for drawing or writing
- develops the directional awareness needed to identify letters and numbers

● You can go on to smaller Double Doodle drawings, using a sheet of paper fastened to a desk or table.

No two-handed drawings on the walls, please!

27

Crossover Dancing School

O.K., all you dancers—here it is. The first Crossover Dancing School, with some great new dances! Whenever you feel tense, nervous, worn out, or unable to concentrate, some good dancing is just the thing you need.

You already know Crossover Dancing from pages 10 and 11 . . . now let's learn some other steps! You can also make up your own dances. The only thing you need to remember is to feel a crisscross pattern to your movements: if you reach out your left arm, then reach out your right leg at the same time, and if you shake your left leg, then shake your right arm, too. So what are we waiting for? Let's start dancing!

Left-Right Tango

Twist-Across

Publications of Edu-Kinesthetics, Inc.

Switching On: The Whole-Brain Answer to Dyslexia
   by Dr. Paul E. Dennison

Edu-K for Kids by Dennison & Dennison

Personalized Whole-Brain Integration by Dennison and Dennison

Brain Gym® by Dennison and Dennison

Brain Gym® Teacher's Edition by Dennison and Dennison

Brain Gym® for Business: Instant Brain Boosters for On-the-Job Success
   by Teplitz, Dennison, and Dennison

The Learning Gym by Erich Ballinger

I Am the Child: Using Brain Gym® with Children Who Have Special Needs
   by Cecilia Freeman and Gail Dennison

Brain Gym® Surfer by Sandra Hinsley

Vision Gym: Playful Movements for Natural Seeing
   (card set and booklet) by Dennison and Dennison

Integrated Movements (audiotape) by Dennison and Dennison

A New Paradigm in Reading Instruction (videotape) with Dr. Paul E.
   Dennison

Hands On: How to Use Brain Gym® in the Classroom
   by Isabel Cohen and Marcelle Goldsmith

Visit our www.braingym.com Web site for
product descriptions and pricing.

Telephone or fax ordering with Visa or MasterCard:
Telephone (805) 650-3303 or toll-free (888) 388-9898
Fax (805) 650-1689

Or mail your order to: Edu-Kinesthetics, Inc., Post Office Box 3395,
Ventura, California 93006-3395, U.S.A.